DEBRA VENABLE

Gold Mining for Fun: A Beginners Guide to Finding Gold

This book was professionally typeset on Reedsy.
Find out more at reedsy.com

Contents

Prologue

The First Spark

It started with a simple idea: what if there's gold right under our feet? I was standing at the edge of a stream, the water sparkling in the sunlight, when I picked up a handful of dirt and gravel. Slowly swirling it in a pan, I saw nothing at first—just mud and small rocks. But then, a tiny glimmer caught my eye and my heart skipped a beat. Could it be?

That moment, no matter how small, changed everything. It wasn't just about the speck of gold; it was the thrill of discovery, the connection to nature, and the thought of following in the footsteps of prospectors from centuries past. Gold mining wasn't just a hobby—it became a passion, an escape, and a way to explore the world around me.

This book is the result of those experiences. A guide to help you uncover your own glimmers of gold—whether they come from a pan, a sluice box, or simply the joy of the search. Because at the end of the day, gold mining isn't just about what you find; it's about the adventure that leads you there.

Introduction

Welcome to the exciting world of recreational gold mining! Whether you're here out of curiosity, a desire to try something new, this book is designed to guide you every step of the way.

Gold mining is more than just a hobby—it's a chance to connect with history, nature, and the timeless thrill of discovery. It's an activity that draws people of all ages, backgrounds, and experience levels to rivers, streams, and hillsides in search of that elusive glint of gold. But don't worry—this isn't about "striking it rich." Instead, it's about finding joy in the process and building memories you'll treasure as much as any gold you might find.

In this guide, you'll find practical advice, tried-and -true techniques, and safety tips to help you get started. We'll explore how to choose the right equipment , select promising locations, and understand different methods like panning, sluicing, and dry mining. Beyond that, you'll learn how to clean and store your findings and perhaps; most importantly, how to embrace the deeper rewards of the search itself.

This book isn't just about techniques; it's about the experience. Gold mining is a journey—one that can take you to beautiful, remote places, teach you patience and resilience, and connect you with a community of like-minded adventurers.

So, whether you're an aspiring prospector or simply looking for a fun outdoor activity, this guide will help you make the most of every moment. Let's get started on your adventure into the fascinating world of gold mining!

1

Recreational Gold Mining:

Recreational gold mining is the modern-day version of an old adventure. People of all ages head out to rivers, creeks, and hillsides, panning , digging for traces of gold that might have been overlooked during earlier gold rushes. While professional miners dig deep with heavy machinery, recreational miners usually stick to small-scale, low-impact techniques like panning, sluicing, and metal detecting, often finding just enough gold to keep the thrill alive.

For many, the joy of recreational mining isn't about getting rich; it is about connecting with history, spending time in nature, and the rush that comes from spotting a glint of gold at the bottom of a pan. Whether you're searching the desert with a metal detector or sifting through river sands with a pan, recreational gold mining combines the thrill of a treasure with an escape into the great outdoors.

Quick History of Gold Mining

Here, provide a brief history of major gold rushes showing how they shaped the world and fueled the "gold fever" that still inspires hobbyists today.

The California Gold Rush (1848-1855)

- In 1848, gold was discovered at Sutter's Mill in California sparking a mass migration. Thousand of hopeful prospectors, known as "49ers," traveled to California by land and sea, seeking fortune in rivers and hillsides.
- "Gold fever" spread like wildfire as news reached the East Coast and even overseas, turning California into a booming economy

and quickly populating the state. Though few struck it rich, the California Gold Rush inspired many future gold-seekers and transformed the American West.

The Klondike Gold Rush (1896—1899)

- The discovery of gold in Canada's remote Yukon Territory in 1896 set off another famous gold rush, known as the Klondike or Yukon Gold Rush. Thousands of prospectors braved harsh winter condition, crossing mountains and rivers to reach the Klondike .
- While this gold rush was short-lived, it's one of the most legendary due to the extreme hardships and the rugged spirit of those who dared the journey. Towns like Dawson City became famous boomtowns and the stories of grit and adventure live on today.

Other Famous Gold Rushes

- Australia also had several notable gold rushes, including those in New South Wales and Victoria in the 1850s, which attracted people from around the world.
- Other gold rushes took place in south Africa, New Zealand, and Alaska, each bringing waves of prospectors hoping to strike it rich.
- These gold rushes changed the world, leading to the founding of cities, the opening of new trade routes, and, ultimately , the rise of recreational gold prospecting as a modern-day pastime.

The Allure of Gold Fever

There's something uniquely thrilling about the possibility of uncovering gold. Whether it's the shine of the nugget in a riverbed or the hope of striking it big, gold fever taps into our natural sense of adventure. For many hobbyists, gold mining is more than just a pastime—it's a journey that combines treasure hunting, outdoor exploration, and the thrill of discovery.

Imagine setting out to a remote stream or hillside, your gear in hand and excitement in your heart. The possibility of finding gold, even a tiny flake, keeps you moving, looking , and searching. It's not just about the metal itself; it's about the pursuit and the mystery of what lies hidden beneath the surface.

A Connection to History

Gold fever isn't a new phenomenon—it's part of our shared history. The famous gold rushes of the 1800s sparked mass migrations, built entire towns, and shaped the culture of regions like California and Alaska. Each gold rush was fueled by stories of instant wealth, but also by dreams and determination. When you go out looking for gold today, you're walking in the footsteps of prospectors who came before you, sharing in that timeless quest.

In many ways, modern recreational gold miners feel a kinship with the 49ers. Klondike miners, and Australian diggers who faced hardships, made discoveries, and sometimes even struck it rich. Gold fever connects you not only to history but also to the spirit of exploration that continues to inspire people today.

The Unpredictable Thrill of the hunt

Gold mining is, at its core, a treasure hunt. You never know what you might find or when you might find it. This unpredictability is a big part of what keeps people coming back. Even experienced prospectors have stories of surprising finds—sometimes in places where they least expected it.

Each time you scoop up a pan of dirt or check your sluice, there's a thrill that keeps your heart racing. Will there be a glint of gold, a shiny flake, or even a small nugget? The "what if" factor is powerful, creating an excitement that's hard to find in everyday life. For many, it's this adrenaline, combined with the joy of being outdoors, that brings them back time and again.

The Gold Itself: A Symbol of Wealth and Beauty

Gold has a mystique all its own. Its rare beauty and lasting value make it one of the world's most prized metals. Even a tiny amount feels precious, and the sight of gold shimmering at the bottom of a pan can be a rewarding experience in itself. Unlike other metals. Gold has been used for currency, art, and jewelry across cultures and ages. For many recreational miners finding even a little bit of gold feels like uncovering a piece of natural treasure.

The physical beauty of gold, with its bright luster and weight, has inspired people throughout history. From ancient Egypt to modern times, gold has been seen as a symbol of wealth, status, and beauty. When you find gold in nature, it's a reminder of its timeless appeal and why so many people have sought it throughout the ages.

Gold Fever Today: A Hobby, a Passion, a Lifestyle

Today's recreational gold mining may not be about building a fortune, but for many hobbyists, it's still a passion–and sometimes even a way of life. Modern–day prospectors come from all walks of life, drawn by the thrill, the connection to history, and the simple pleasure of spending time outdoors. Some travel to remote locations, others explore local rivers, and a few even dedicate their vacations to mining sites across the country.

Gold fever today isn't about greed or getting rich; it's about connecting with the land, the past, and the thrill of exploration. It's a chance to disconnect from the modern world and experience something timeless and real. For those who catch gold fever, the journey is as meaningful as any piece of gold they might find.

2

Tools and Equipment for Gold Mining

Recreational gold mining doesn't require a huge investment in tools. In fact, part of the appeal is that you can do it with just a few basic tools and some know-how, you'll be ready to start exploring for gold in no time. Where you're panning along a riverbank or setting up a sluice box, , these simple tools can

help you uncover hidden treasures. Here's a rundown of the essential tools and some extras for those ready to take it a step further.

The Essentials: Basic tools for Every Prospector

Gold Pan

The gold pan is the classic tool of the trade. Made of plastic or metal, it's a shallow, round pan that helps you separate, gold from sand, gravel, and other materials. Pan come in various sizes, usually between 10 to 16 inches in diameter, and with different riffles (small ridges) long the edge to trap gold particles. For beginners, a medium-size pan with some riffles is ideal.

The gold pan is where it all begins. Using it is simple: scoop a small amount of dirt or gravel, add water, and swirl it gently. The key is to keep the heavier particles, like gold, at the bottom while lighter material is washed away. Beginners might want to practice at home with dirt and small pebbles before trying it in a real stream, just to get a feel for the swirling motion. Some prospectors even start with two pans of different sizes–one larger for initial material and a smaller one for more concentrated samples.

Hand Shovel

A hand shovel or trowel makes digging easier, whether you're collecting gravel from a riverbed or digging in drier areas. Look for a model with a comfortable grip, especially if you'll be working for hours.Some prospectors recommend a foldable shovel, which is easier to carry in a backpack. For wetter environments,a small plastic scoop (like a garden scoop) works well and won't rust.

Classifiers

Classifiers help you sift out unwanted rocks and large debris, letting you focus on the smaller particles that might contain gold. Classifiers fit over your pan, so you can shovel material directly into them, shake,and let the fines drop through. For a finer classifier, you can use a second screen with an even smaller mesh size (⅛ inch). This process helps save time by reducing the amount of unnecessary material in your pan.

Vibrating Classifiers

In more advanced setups, a vibrating classifier or sieve can sort materials by size before they go through the dry washer. This helps concentrate gold-bearing material and reduces the amount of waste.

Upgrading Your Toolkit: Sluice Boxes, Metal Detectors,and More

Sluice Box

A sluice box allows you to process more materials than a pan alone. Here's how it works: place the sluice in a shallow part of a stream with enough flow to carry away lighter gravel but not so strong that it disturbs the sluice. The water should flow over the riffles, which trap heavier particles like gold. For best results, set the sluice at a slight angle (about one inch drop per foot of sluice length) and add material gradually. Be sure to check the riffles periodically for any gold particles that might be caught there.

Tip: Look for a lightweight, portable sluice box if you're prospecting remote areas. Many sluices have removable riffles or built-in mats that catch fine gold, making cleanup easier.

Tools and Techniques for Dry Mining

- **Dry Washers:** The main piece of equipment for dry mining, dry washers use air instead of water to separate gold from other materials. They come various sizes and types, but the basic concept is the same:

- A dry washer has a box with a screen that allows air to blow up from the bottom.
- Material is fed into the top, and as it shakes and bounces, lighter material blows away, leaving the heavier gold to settle.

Metal Detectors: Metal Detectors are a popular tool for dry mining because they can help locate gold nuggets or larger particles under the surface without digging up large amounts of soil. Metal detectors takes some practice to get right, but it's a rewarding way to explore new places. Look for a metal detector designed for gold prospecting, as these are more sensitive to the small particles of metal you're likely to find. Practice listening to the subtle sounds of your detector, and remember to dig every signal when you,re learning, as different metals produce slightly different tones. Many detectors allow you to adjust sensitivity and discrimination settings to ignore certain metals, making it easier to focus on gold.

Tip: Bring a small digging tool specifically for metal detecting to quickly check promising spots without disturbing too much soil.

Additional Accessories and Tips

Snuffer Bottle

A snuffer bottle is a small plastic bottle with a nozzle used to suck up fine gold particles from your pan. After you're finished panning, use the snuffer bottle to carefully pick up any gold trapped in crevices or at the bottom of the pan. This keeps your gold safely stored until you're ready to clean it.

Magnifying Loupe

A magnifying loupe helps you closely examine any small particles or flakes in your pan. This can be especially helpful if you're unsure whether a shiny fleck is actually gold or just fool's gold(pyrite). Loupes with 10x magnification are a good choice, as they're compact and provide clear detail.

Storage Vials or Containers

Once you're collected some gold, even a small vial can be a fun way to store and display your finds. Look for small glass or plastic vials with screw-on caps. For any larger nuggets or interesting specimens, you might want a larger, clear container. These make great keepsakes and conversation pieces.

With this set of tools and a few helpful accessories, you're ready to begin your prospecting journey. Each tool plays a unique role, and as you gain experience, you'll discover your own preferences and techniques. Starting small and building your toolkit over time makes recreational gold mining a hobby you can grow into, whether you're prospecting once a year or every weekend.

3

Techniques for Finding Gold

old prospecting offers a range of techniques, each suited to different locations and conditions. Whether you're by a river, in the desert, or in a gold-rich area, these can help you maximize your chances of finding that gleam of gold.

Panning: The Classic Method

Panning is one of the simplest and most iconic gold prospecting techniques. Ideal for beginners and easily practiced in rivers and streams, panning requires only a gold pan, patience, and a bit of practice.

Steps of Panning:

- **Gather Material**
- Begin by filling your pan with material from a promising spot in the river or stream. Look for areas where gold might settle, like behind rocks, in small river bends, or in slow-moving water.
- **Add Water and Shake**

- Submerge the pan in water and shake it side to side. This motion helps gold, which is heavier than other materials, sink to the bottom of the pan.
- **Swirl and Tilt**
- Tilt the pan slightly and swirl it gently. As you do this, allow the lighter materials to wash over the edge, keeping an eye on what remains in the bottom.
- **Check for Gold**
- Continue swirling until you have only a small amount of material left. Look closely at the bottom of the pan; if you're lucky, you'll spot tiny flakes or specks of gold. Use a snuffer bottle to collect any gold particles.

Tips for Success:

- Start with a medium-size pan, as it's easier to control for beginners.
- Take your time—panning can be repetitive, but patience pays off.
- Practice panning at home with sand or gravel before heading to the river to build confidence.

Sluicing: Increasing Efficiency with Running Water

For those wanting to process more material than a pan alone, a sluice box is an excellent tool. Using the power of running water, a sluice helps separate gold from other material more quickly.

Here's a guide to building a simple, effective sluice box for gold mining using basic materials.

Gather Materials

- **Wood or Aluminum:** For the sluice box frame. Wood is easy to work with, but aluminum is lightweight, durable, and won't warp if it gets wet.
- **Riffles:** You can make these from metal strips or wooden dowels. they help trap the gold as water flows over them.
- **Rubber mat or Miners' Moss:** This is laid on the bottom of the sluice box under the riffles to catch fine gold particles
- **Mesh Screen:** To classify or filter material by size.
- **Screws or Rivets:** For securing the frame and riffles.
- **Silicone or Epoxy Glue:** To seal any gaps and help waterproof the box if you use wood.
- **Hinges(optional):** If you want to make a foldable sluice for portability.

Determine the Size

The typical sluice box for recreational use is about 24-48 inches long, 10-12 inches wide, and 4-6 inches deep. Adjust the size based on your needs and the area where you'll be mining.

Build the Frame

- **Cut the Wood or Aluminum :** Cut two long side panels, and two shorter pieces, for the front and back.
- **Assemble:** Use screws or rivets to attach the sides, front, and back pieces. Ensure the bottom of the box is flat and secure.
- **Seal (for Wood):** Use silicone or epoxy to seal the joints inside the box to prevent water leaks.

Install the Riffles

- **Measure and Mark:** Evenly space the riffles, leaving about 1-2 inches between each one. The riffles should be oriented so that water flows over them, creating a small area of turbulence that helps trap gold.
- **Attach the Riffles:** Screw or rivets each riffle into place across the bottom of the sluice box.
- **Adjust the Angle:** Angle the riffles at about 45 degrees to the bottom of the sluice box to encourage gold to settle behind each riffle.

Add the Mat or Miners' Moss

- **Lay it Down:** Place a rubber mat or miners' moss at the bottom of the sluice box under the riffles. This matting helps capture fine gold particles that might otherwise flow through the box.
- **Secure the Mat:** Use adhesive or small screws to keep the mat in place, especially near the edges.

Attach a Classifying Screen (Optional)

Adding a screen above the sluice can help prevent larger rocks from clogging the box. The screen can be secured with screws or a removable setup if you'd like to clean it periodically.

Steps for Sluicing:

- **Choose a Good Spot**
- Look for a section of the stream with moderate flow, enough to carry lighter materials out of the sluice but not too forceful. Position the sluice box so the water flows directly through it.

- **Set the Angle**
- Place the sluice at a slight angle, around one inch of drop per foot of sluice length. This allows gold to settle in the riffles as lighter material is washed out
- **Add Material**
- Feed small shovelful of material into the top of the sluice. The water will carry lighter material down, while heavier particles, including gold, settle behind the riffles.
- **Clean Out the Sluice**
- Periodically, remove the sluice from the water and check the riffles for any trapped gold. Carefully remove the mats or riffles to capture the gold, then reset the sluice to continue.

Tips for Success:

- Use classifiers to screen out larger rocks, allowing the sluice to focus on smaller, gold-bearing material.
- Regularly clean the sluice, especially after a productive section of river, to maximize your yield.
- Experiment with different angles and water speeds for the best results.

Dry Panning: Techniques for Desert Prospecting

Dry panning is ideal for arid areas where water is scarce. While it's more challenging than traditional panning, dry panning can still yield results in gold-rich deserts.

Steps for Dry Panning:

1. Gather Dry Material

Collect dry soil or gravel from gold-bearing areas, like old riverbeds or desert washes. Look for spots where heavy minerals might concentrate, such as dips or natural catchments.

2. Shake and Tilt

Similar to wet panning, dry panning involves shaking the material to let heavy particles sink to the bottom. Shake the pan vigorously to encourage this separation.

3. Blow Away Lighter Material

After shaking, gently blow across the pan to remove lighter material from the top. Be careful not to blow too hard, or you might lose potential gold particles as well.

4. Examine for Gold

Continue shaking and blowing until only the heaviest particles remain. Examine the pan closely for flecks of gold, especially in the crevices and lower edges.

Tips for Success:

- A light breeze can assist with dry panning, helping to remove finer dust without disturbing heavier particles.
- Practice is key, as it can be harder to control the material in dry conditions.
- If available, a small brush can help sweep away light dust, leaving only the heavier particles behind.

How to Use A Dry Washer

Using a dry washer requires a bit of setup, but it's straightforward once you're familiar with the process:

- **Find a Location:** Look for places where gold is likely to have accumulated, such as dry riverbeds, washes, or gulches. Gold tends to settle in lower areas where heavier particles naturally collect.

- **Set Up the Dry Washer**: Position the dry washer on a stable surface, ideally at a slight angle so that material flows smoothly from top to bottom. The exact angle will vary depending on the model and soil conditions, but 10-15 degrees is typical.
- **Feed Material:** Add dry material (gravel,sand, and dirt) into the hopper. The machine will create a steady airflow and vibration to help separate the lighter particles from the heavier gold.
- **Collect Gold**: As lighter materials blow away, gold and other heavy minerals settle into a riffle tray or another collection area. Periodically empty the tray to ensure it doesn't overflow, and store any gold you recover.

Tips for Success In Dry Mining

- **Pick the Right Time:** Dry mining works best when soil is completely dry. After a rainstorm, it may take several days for materials to dry enough for the dry washer to work effectively.
- **Look for Natural Traps:** Just like with wet panning. gold often gets caught in crevices, behind rocks, or in areas where the wind has concentrated heavier particles.
- **Avoid Clay-Rich Areas:** Clay can make dry mining difficult because it's sticky and doesn't sift well though the dry washer. Aim for sandy, loose soils with a mix of small rocks and gravel.

Dry mining can be a rewarding and adventurous way to find gold, especially in arid environments. Whether you're working with a dry washer, metal detector, or simple hand tools, dry mining lets you explore and enjoy the thrill of treasure hunting where water mining wouldn't be possible!

Each of these techniques brings a different approach to the search for gold. Whether you're near water, working with a sluice, or in the desert with just a pan, these methods allow you to adapt to various conditions and locations.

4

Choosing the Right Location

inding the right location is crucial to gold mining success. While luck plays a role, experienced prospectors know that choosing a good spot requires research, knowledge of geological clues, and sometimes even permission from local authorities. This chapter will walk you through the steps to find the best possible locations to start your search.

Understanding Gold-Bearing Areas

Gold doesn't appear just anywhere—it tends to concentrate in specific type of geological areas. Knowing what to look for can help you identify promising spots.

Where Gold is Found

- **Streams and Rivers:** Gold often collects in stream and riverbeds due to erosion. Look for spots along bends in the river, around large rocks, and in areas where the water flow slows.
- **Old River Channels:** Sometimes, gold can be found in dry riverbeds, especially if the river has shifted over time.
- **Quartz Veins and Bedrock:** Gold is often found alongside quartz and in cracks in bedrock.If you're in an area with visible bedrock, inspect crevices and cracks where gold may have settled.

Tip: You don't have to be a geologist, but understanding basic geology can go a long way. Learn to spot signs of gold-bearing rocks and minerals, like quartz, black sand, and sulfide minerals, which often occur with gold.

2. Researching Locations: Maps, Guides, and Online Resources

Before you even step outside, a little research can help you narrow down your options. Knowing where gold has been found in the past can increase your chances of success.

Using Maps and Historical Data

- **Mining Maps and Reports:** Look up maps and historical reports that show known gold deposits. Many areas with historical mining activity are still accessible for recreational mining today.
- **Topographic Maps:** These maps show natural features like hills, valleys, and waterways, which can help you identify potential gold-bearing locations. Waterways and low areas are often good places to start.

Online Tools and Resources

- **BLM and USGS Websites:** In the U.S., the Bureau of Land Management (BLM) and the United States Geological Survey (USGS) offer resources and maps of public lands where recreational mining is allowed. These sites also provide geological maps and information on mineral resources.
- **Gold Mining Forums and Community Groups:** Online prospecting communities can provide up-to-date information on promising areas, conditions, and tips from other prospectors. Many experienced hobbyists enjoy sharing tips on current "hot spots" and gold-friendly locations.

Identifying High-Potential Spots Within Your Location

Once you're on-site, there are some signs and areas to look for that can improve your chances of finding gold.

Streams Locations

- **Inside Bends:** Look for bends in a stream where the water slows down. Gold, being heavy, is more likely to settle in these spots.

- **Behind Large Rocks and Boulders:** When water flows around obstacles, it creates eddies where gold particles can accumulate.
- **Gravel Bars:** These deposits, found in the middle or along the sides of streams, can be gold-rich due to sediment accumulation over time.

Dry Areas

- **Dry Riverbeds:** In arid regions, dry riverbeds, called "washes," are often gold-bearing. Look for small catchment areas or depressions where gold particles may have settled.
- **Bench Deposits:** These are ancient riverbeds now above the current river level, often found along hillside near a river.

Tip: Don't overlook the "pay streak"-a section of stream or riverbed where gold has accumulated over time. Pay streaks often follow a line along the bedrock beneath the stream.

4. Respecting Regulations and Gaining Permission

Not all land is open to prospecting, so be sure to follow local laws and guidelines.

Public Lands and Designated Areas

- **BLM and National Forests:** In the U.S., much of the gold prospecting occurs on public lands managed by the BLM or National Forest Service. Check their regulations, as some areas are open for recreational mining, while others are not.

- **Recreational Gold Mining Sites:** Some regions have designated areas specifically for recreational gold mining. These are often well-mapped and include areas with historical gold activity.

Private Property and Claims

- **Private Property:** Always get permission before prospecting on private land. Some landowners are open to allowing recreational miners, but permission is essential.
- **Existing Claim:** Prospecting on an active claim is illegal without the claim holder's permission. Check claim maps or contact local authorities to ensure you're in a legal spot.

Tip: Prospecting responsibly not only protects the environment but also supports local rules that allow public access to gold-bearing lands. It's always a good practice to "leave no trace" and follow ethical prospecting guidelines.

By taking the time to research and carefully choose your prospecting location, you're setting yourself up for success. Each gold-bearing area has unique features and challenges, but with these tips. You'll be well-equipped to find a promising spot that gives you the best possible chance to uncover gold.

5

Safely Considerations

While gold mining can be a fun and rewarding activity, it's important to stay aware of safety risks and to follow best practices for a safe outing. In this chapter, we'll cover some essential safety tips, from physical protection in the outdoors to environmental care.

Preparing for the Outdoors

Before you even start digging or panning, preparation is key to ensuring a safe experience.

Essential Gear and Clothing

- **Appropriate Clothing:** Wear long sleeves, sturdy pants, and hiking boots. This will help protect against weather, insects, and any rough or rocky terrain.
- **Protective Gloves and Eye Protection:** Use gloves to handle rocks and equipment, and consider eye protection especially if using a hammer or pick on hard surfaces.
- **Water and Food:** Bring enough water and snacks for the day. Dehydration and fatigue can sneak up quickly, especially in hot or remote areas.

First Aid Kit

- **Basic First Aid Supplies:** A portable kit with bandages, antiseptic wipes, tweezers and pain relievers is essential.
- **Bug Spray and Sunscreen:** Mosquitoes and sun exposure can be a major nuisance, so be prepared with bug spray and high-SPF sunscreen.

Tip: Let someone know where you'll be prospecting, especially if it's a remote location, and keep a map or GPS with you.

2. Hazards in Water and on Land

Depending on where you're prospecting, you may encounter unique hazards, so stay aware of your surroundings.

Water Safety for Panning and Sluicing

- **Be Aware of Water Depth and Flow:** Even shallow water can be dangerous if the current is strong. Choose areas with a stable flow, and avoid fast-moving streams or rivers.
- **Non-Slip Footwear:** Rocks in streams can be slippery. Wear shoes with good traction, and be careful stepping in areas where you can't see the bottom clearly.
- **Weather Awareness:** Flash floods can occur suddenly in certain areas, especially after rain. Always be aware of weather conditions and be prepared to leave if the water level rises unexpectedly.

Land Hazard for Dry Mining

- **Watch for Loose Rock and Soil:** In dry areas, loose soil or rock can create tripping hazards or even minor rockslides. Always test the stability of the ground before digging.
- **Be Cautious on Hillsides:** If prospecting on a slope, work slowly and carefully. Avoid steep areas where rocks could shift unexpectedly.
- **Wildlife Awareness:** Many remote areas are home to wildlife. Be

mindful of snakes, insects, and large animals, and avoid disturbing their habitats.

Tip: Always stay alert and plan your steps carefully, especially in unfamiliar terrain.

3. Handling Equipment Safely

Even basic prospecting tools require care to avoid injury.

Using Picks, Shovels, and Sluices

- **Proper Technique with Tools:** Use a stable, controlled grip when swinging a pick or shovel, and take breaks to prevent fatigue. If working with heavy rocks, lift with your legs, not your back.
- **Setting Up a Sluice Safely:** When placing a sluice in the water, make sure it's stable to avoid unexpected shifting. Position it away from areas with heavy foot traffic to prevent accidents.

Avoiding Repetitive Strain

- **Take Regular Breaks:** Mining can be physically demanding. Stop and rest to prevent strains and injuries, particularly when lifting or shoveling.
- **Switch Up Tasks:** Alternate between activities like panning, digging and setting up equipment to give different muscle groups a break.

Tip: Stretch before and after mining to help prevent soreness and injury.

4. Environmental Safety and Ethics

Responsible prospecting isn't just about physical safety; it's also about protecting the natural surroundings.

Respect Local Wildlife and Vegetation

- **Stay on Established Paths:** Avoid creating new paths, which can damage fragile ecosystems and disrupt local wildlife.
- **Don't Disturb Animals or Nests:** Be cautious if you see animal tracks, nests, or signs of activity. Give wildlife plenty of space, and leave habitats undisturbed.

Leave No Trace

- **Pack Out What You Bring In:** Take all trash, tools, and equipment with you. Avoid leaving any items behind.
- **Limit Digging Impact:** Keep holes small and fill them in when you're done. Large holes can create hazards for other people and animals.

Follow Local Regulations

Observe Mining Laws and Guidelines: In addition to keeping you legal, respecting local rules helps maintain access to public lands for future prospectors.

Respect Claim Boundaries: If you're near a mining claim, avoid disturbing the area without permission. Many claims are clearly marked, but when in doubt, check maps or ask local authorities.

Tip: Always leave the area better than you found it. Responsible prospecting helps preserve nature and keeps recreational areas open for everyone.

5. Staying Alert and Knowing When to Stop

Perhaps the best safety tip of all is to know your limits. If conditions become unsafe,
  It's always best to pack up and head home.

Weather Changes

- **Monitor the Sky:** Weather can change quickly, especially in mountainous or desert areas. If storms roll in, it's wise to call it a day and head to safety.

Personal Limits

- **Listen to Your Body:** Mining can be hard work, so don't push past your comfort zone. If you're feeling tired or dehydrated, take a break or end the day early.

Remember, no amount of gold is worth sacrificing your safety. By staying alert and prepared, you'll enjoy many safe and successful outings.

6

Cleaning and Storing your Finds

Once you've had a successful outing and gathered some gold or interesting rocks, the next step is to clean and store them properly. This chapter covers basic cleaning techniques, how to handle delicate pieces, and ideas for safely storing and displaying your treasures.

Cleaning Gold and Other Finds

Cleaning gold is fairly straightforward, but other types of rocks or minerals may need extra care to avoid damage.

Basic Cleaning for Gold

- **Remove Dirt and Sediment:** Use a soft brush (like a toothbrush) with warm water to gently scrub any dirt or sediment off your gold. Avoid using harsh chemicals, as gold is sensitive to certain acids and cleaners.
- **Polishing:** If you want to give your gold a bit of shine, you can gently polish it with a soft cloth. Avoid anything abrasive as it could scratch the surface of the gold.

Cleaning Rocks and Artifacts

- **Soaking in Water:** For most rocks and minerals, a soak in water can loosen dirt and make them easier to clean. Use a toothbrush to scrub delicate spots.
- **Avoiding Chemicals:** Some rocks are sensitive to household cleaners and may get damaged. When in doubt, use only water and a soft brush.

Tip: For delicate or rare stones, consult a rock-cleaning guide or professional to avoid damage.

Storing Your Gold and Rock Finds

Proper storage keeps your finds in good condition and makes it easy too revisit your collection over time.

Storage Tips for Gold

Small Containers or Bags: Gold flakes and nuggets are best stored in small, individual containers or zip-lock bags to prevent scratches.

Labeling Finds: Label your containers with details like the location and date, which can be fun for tracking your progress and memories.

Storing Rocks and Artifacts

- **Dividers or Foam Pads:** For fragile or valuable rocks, consider using a container with foam dividers to keep pieces from knocking together.
- **Climate Control:** Avoid storing rocks in damp areas, as moisture can sometimes lead to corrosion or mold on certain types of minerals.

Displaying Your Treasures

If you'd like to show off your finds, there are many creative ways to display them without compromising their quality.

Display ideas for Gold

- **Shadow Boxes:** Display small gold nuggets or flakes in a shadow box, where they can be viewed easily but are still protected.
- **Coin Capsules:** For small gold pieces, coin capsules or similar clear containers can showcase your finds while keeping them secure.

Creative Displays for Rocks and Artifacts

- **Specimen Frames:** These frames hold rocks or minerals securely, allowing you to arrange multiple pieces for display.
- **Jewelry:** If you find a unique or beautiful stone, consider having it made into a necklace or ring.

Tip: For valuable or delicate pieces, keep them out of direct sunlight, as UV rays can sometimes cause colors to fade.

4.Cataloging Your Collection

Keeping track of what you've found adds a rewarding layer to your prospecting hobby and helps you keep a record of your progress.

Cataloging Tips

- **Notebook or Digital App:** Use a notebook or app to log each outing, including notes on where you searched and what you found. Photos are also a great addition.
- **Adding Details:** Record information like the size, weight, or location of each find. Over time, this log can become a valuable reference and a fun part of your journey.

7

The Joy of the Search: Why it's not all about the Gold

F*or many who take up recreational gold mining, the thrill goes beyond the prospect of finding gold. It's about the journey itself– the peaceful moments in nature, the excitement of discovery, and the sense of*

stepping into history. This chapter explores the joys of the search, reminding us why gold mining is rewarding even when the gold itself is scarce.

Rediscovering Nature

Being outdoors is one of the biggest reasons people are drawn to gold mining. It offers an escape from everyday life and a chance to reconnect with the natural world.

Connecting with the Land

- **Natural Beauty:** Gold mining takes you to beautiful rivers, mountains and forests that might be missed in regular life.The natural scenery and quiet sounds of flowing water or rustling trees become part of the joy.
- **Learning Local Wildlife:** As you search for gold, you may spot different animals, plants,and unique geological features, making each trip feel like a mini-adventure in nature.

Escaping the Routine

- **Mindfulness on the Moment:** Panning for gold is a slow, rhythmic activity that allows you to focus on the here and now. For many, it's a form of mindfulness that provides a break from daily stresses and technology.
- **Time in Solitude or with Friends:** Whether you're prospecting alone or with friends there's a deep satisfaction in spending time in nature, far from the usual routines.

The Thrill of Discovery

Even when you don't strike it rich, there's a sense of excitement in the search itself.

The Potential for Surprise

- **You Never Know What You'll Find:** Sometimes, the reward is a unique rock or an unusual artifact that wasn't part of the plan. Each discovery, big or small, adds to the joy of prospecting.
- **Treasure Hunt Feel:** There's a timeless thrill to the search, much like a treasure hunt, that taps into a deep sense of adventure. It's a reminder of stories and legends of hidden riches and the dream of uncovering something valuable.

Building Skills and Knowledge

- **Becoming a Better Prospector:** Each trip builds your skills, whether it's spotting geological signs, learning about new equipment or gaining the patience to keep trying. Over time, you become more knowledgeable and experienced, and each success feels even more rewarding.
- **Understanding the History of Mining:** Prospecting also offers a chance to step into the past, experiencing a bit of what early miners felt. It's a tangible way to connect with history and appreciate the trials and excitement of those who came before.

Finding Peace in Patience

Gold prospecting is rarely a quick success. Learning to be patient is one of the greatest gifts it offers.

The Value of Persistence

- **Embracing the Slow Pace:** Unlike other fast-paced hobbies, gold mining requires time and persistence. Learning to enjoy the slower process of searching and sifting builts patience and resilience.
- **The Joy in Small Successes:** When you find even the smallest flake of gold after a long search, it feels like a big win. This teaches the value of persistence and makes every find, no matter how small, feel significant.

A Lesson in Resilience

- **Accepting the Unknown:** Gold mining can be unpredictable. Learning to accept that you may come up empty-handed teaches resilience and a willingness to embrace the process over the outcome.
- **Learning from Each Attempt:** Every outing, successful or not teaches something new. Maybe you found a better spot, learned how to read the landscape, or simply gained a memory of a beautiful day outdoors.

The Lasting Rewards Beyond Gold

Ultimately, the greatest rewards in recreational gold mining often come from the experience, not the material gain.

Stories and Memories

- **Sharing Your Adventures:** Each outing creates stories to share with family, friends or fellow prospectors. The memories of scenic views, unexpected finds, and lessons learned become part of your story.
- **Bonding Through the Experience:** Prospecting can be a wonderful way to bond with friends or family, creating lasting memories and shared experiences that deepen relationships.

A Hobby to Pass Down

- **Inspiring Others:** Many prospectors find joy in teaching others, whether it's introducing a friend to panning or passing the hobby on to the next generation. It's a way of keeping the adventure alive for others to enjoy.
- **A Lifelong Pursuit:** Unlike other hobbies, gold prospecting is something you can return to throughout your life. Each new season and each location brings something unique, allowing you to keep finding joy in the search, time and again.

In the end, recreational gold mining offers an experience that goes beyond wealth. It's about reconnecting with nature, enjoying the thrill of discovery, and embracing patience and resilience. Whether you find gold or not, the journey itself is a priceless reward.

8

Encouragement to Get Started, Final Thoughts

You've now explored the basics of recreational gold mining, from understanding the allure of gold fever to choosing a location, mastering techniques, and keeping safety in mind. But the journey really begins when you pick up your pan and start your own search. In this final chapter, we'll give you some encouragement to take that first step and offer a few final thoughts to keep in mind as you head out.

Taking the First Step

Getting started is easier than you might think! The excitement of gold mining doesn't require a huge investment or extensive experience–just a willingness to explore.

Don't Wait for the "Perfect" Time

- **Start Small:** You don't need to wait until you have all the gear or an ideal location. Start with simple equipment like a pan and some sturdy boots. Even a local stream or nearby public land can be a great place to begin.

- **Learn as You Go:** There's no need to know everything up front. The best lessons come from trying things firsthand, seeing what works, and building your knowledge along the way.

Embrace the Adventure

- **Enjoy Each Step:** Remember, prospecting is about enjoying the journey. Whether you're panning in a river, working a sluice, or trying your hand at dry mining, each trip will bring new sights, challenges, and small successes.
- **Bring a Friend:** Consider inviting a friend or family member along. Sharing the adventure makes it even more fun, and it's a great way to make memories together.

Keeping a Positive Mindset

Prospecting requires patience, and it's easy to get discouraged if the gold doesn't show up right away. Here's how to keep a positive outlook as you learn.

Celebrate the Process

- **Find Joy Beyond the Gold:** As we discussed in Chapter 7, the rewards of prospecting aren't just about gold. Appreciate the beauty of your surroundings, the thrill of discovery, and the knowledge that you're following in the footsteps of history.
- **Set Small Goals:** Rather than focusing on big finds , set smaller

goals for each outing.

- For example, aim to improve your panning technique, learn more about reading the landscape, or simply spend an enjoyable day outdoors.

Remember You're Part of a Legacy

- **A Timeless Hobby:** Recreational gold mining connects you to centuries of history and the spirit of exploration. Whether you find gold or not, you're part of a tradition that's as much about passion and curiosity as it is about riches.

Final Tips and Thought

Before you head out, here are a few final pieces of advice to keep in mind as you begin your journey.

Stay Safe and Respect the Land

- **Protect Yourself and the Environment:** Always prioritize safety, from wearing the right gear to observing local regulations. Respect the environment by following Leave No Trace principles, and ensure that the land remains open and beautiful for future prospectors.

Be Open to Learning

- **Ask for Advice:** Don't hesitate to reach out to other hobbyists. Joining prospecting communities,reading guides, and learning from other's experiences can make your journey more rewarding.

- **Reflect on Your Progress:** Keep a log of your outings, noting where you searched and what you found. Over time, this record will reflect your progress, and you may even discover patterns that help you improve.

Your Journey Awaits

Gold prospecting is a rewarding hobby, filled with unexpected discoveries and a deep connection to the natural world. So take a deep breath, grab your pan, and step into the adventure that awaits. The gold may be out there—or maybe it's the memories and lessons along the way that will prove to be your greatest finds.

" With a few flecks of gold tucked in my pocket, I headed back, dirt-streaked and exhausted but smiling. They say gold fever never really leaves you, and maybe they're right. I'll be back. After all, who knows what treasure might still be waiting just around the next bend?" " Happy Prospecting !"

9

Resources

Resources

Bilani N, Benson AB III. Panning for gold in a dry creek?—the ongoing search for role of immunotherapy in mismatch repair proficient rectal cancer. AME Clinical Trials Review. 2024;2:81. doi:10.21037/actr-24-79

Romaine G. Gold panning the Pacific Northwest: A Guide to the Area's Best Sites for Gold. Rowman & Littlefield; 2023.

Ralph C. Fists full of gold.; 2010.

Koch AG. Gold prospecting & placer deposits: Finding Gold Made Simpler. Adam Gregory Koch; 2013.

Forests and Woodlands | Bureau of Land Management. https://www.blm.gov/programs/natural-resources/forests-and-woodlands.

Gold Prospectors Association of America > Home. https://www.goldprospectors.org/.

10

Conclusion

The Journey Begins

Congratulations— you've reached the end of this guide, but your journey is just beginning. Recreational gold mining is more than a hobby; it's an adventure waiting to happen . Whether you're standing at the edge of a stream, hiking through rugged terrain, or sifting soil in a desert wash, every step brings the thrill of discovery and the joy of exploring the great outdoors.

Remember, gold mining isn't just about finding gold. It's about the memories you make, the connections you build with nature, and the satisfaction of learning something new. Each outing will teach you more about the land, the process, and yourself.

I hope this book has given you the tools, knowledge, and inspiration to start your own adventure. From panning your first stream to embracing the deeper joys of the search, you now have everything you need to take the first step.

A Quick Request

If you enjoyed this book or found it helpful, I'd love to hear your thoughts! Your review means the world to me—not only does it help me grow as a writer, but it also helps other readers discover this book, reviews are like gold nuggets to authors, and I thank you for sharing yours.

Final Thoughts

So grab your pan, gather your gear, and step into the world of gold mining with an open mind and a sense of adventure. The gold is out there—but even if it's not, the journey is always worth it.

Wishing you success and golden
memories.
Debra Venable